Thank you for buying this
oring Book! We came up v
where we shared the offic

We're guessing that's why you bought this book because either
you or someone you love has also suffered through hearing too
many of these sayings, too often.

We hope you or your recipient finds this to be a fun, laugh
inducing, passive aggressive way to take out all the angst and
annoyance at the clichés that have taken over too many office
meetings, conference calls, memos and more. This isn't just an
awesome coloring book. We feel we're doing our part to help
save you from the long term, mind-numbing effects of hearing
these clichés on a daily basis.

To make this more than just a coloring book, we've provided
"corporate definitions," fun trivia and a hashtag on the back
of the pages so you can post photos of your artwork on social
media. And most of these pages are workplace friendly so you
can tack them onto your cubicle wall without your manager or
boss giving you the stink eye - well, depending on where you
work that is! *[Disclaimer: we don't make any promises as to whether
your boss or manager will give you the stink eye: you assume the risk!]*.

If you bought this as a gift, we even have a little checklist you
can fill out so you don't have to get a separate card. You can
be cheap and environmentally conscious at the same time!
Hmmm, you may want to make sure your recipient avoids
reading that last sentence – color over it or put a happy sticker
over the word "cheap" (or use some liquid paper if you have
any on hand). Have fun and remember, always be moving
forward!

John, Jenn and Brian

bemovingforward.com/coloringbook

CHECKLIST

I bought this Corporate Clichés Adult Coloring Book for:

☐ Me, myself and I
☒ You, *Barb*_____, because you're the best
and I think you're awesome!
☐ Whoever the recipient of the Secret Santa, White Elephant or Other Anonymous gift giving occasion or party is. Aren't you lucky!

Because:

☐ Hey, I deserve it!
☐ It's your birthday! Happy Birthday, _____!!!
☒ Merry / Happy (circle one) *Christmas*_____ (insert holiday or occasion)!!!
☐ It's my clever contribution to:

  ☐ The Office Holiday Party
  ☐ The Secret Santa Gift Exchange
  ☐ White Elephant Gift Exchange
  ☐ Other _____

– *Your pal Jen* 😊

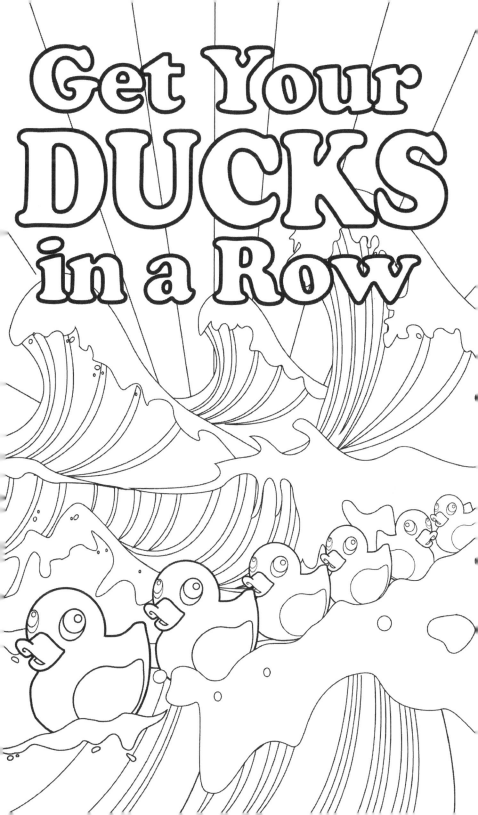

Get your ducks in a row

A call or mandate for organization and order.

The phrase may have originated from the early 1900s from the game of pool when balls are lined up on a pool table. Alternatively, it may have come from duck hunting.

#ducksinarow

Thrown
under the bus

Thrown under the bus

An act of deceit to gain one's trust only to later betray it. Alternatively, to distance oneself from someone when that person's reputation has been damaged. Considered a self-serving and cowardly act.

Its exact origins are unclear though according to Wikipedia one of its earliest uses may have been from a 1984 Washington Post article about Cyndi Lauper, discussing how tough the music industry is.

#underthebus

Synergy

Combining efforts, skills and talents to produce a greater result or outcome.

In biochemistry and pharmacology, synergy refers to the combined effect of two or more drugs or stimuli. The word originates from the Latin and Greek word, "synergia" which translates into "joint work." Today, it is one of the most overused and overhyped words in memos, meetings and corporate retreats.

#synergy

Get your manager's blessing

*To obtain clearance or authorization on a
project, request or course of action.*

This one seems to be on every major business publication's top annoying or "please stop saying this" list. Taking a sacred act that has deep ecumenical roots and likening it to a manager signing off on an expense report is not only cliché, it's sacrilege!

#managersblessing

Ping me!

A request for an email or text message - usually said during situations when a topic cannot be fully discussed at the moment.

A ping was a sonar pulse used as a signal between naval ships. The word was later expanded to IT and network administrators, who used it to refer to the act of checking to see if an internet protocol network was active or online.

#pingme

Not enough bandwidth

Lacking sufficient time, energy or resources to take on additional projects or assignments at work.

"Not enough bandwidth" refers to insufficient network speeds or capacity to handle large downloads on a computer's modem or router. Like "ping me," this is another phrase from the IT world that has been co-opted for wider, eye-roll inducing uses in corporate America.

#notenoughbandwidth

Perrrfect

Free from blemishes or imperfections - an ideal standard or level that is theoretically impossible to attain. The addition of multiple "r's" provides a sleazy, casual, nonchalant tone that lazy managers will sometimes provide to exaggerate their affirmation or pleasure.

The Perfect Storm is a 2000 film, directed by Wolfgang Peterson, starring George Clooney and adapted from the 1997 book by Sebastian Junger. The film is an account of the Andrea Gail fishing vessel that was lost in what was called "1991 Perfect Storm" or "The No-Name Storm." The phrase "perfect storm" is also overused as a cliché both in corporate America and in politics, to describe a tense escalating situation.

#perrrfect

Think outside the box

To think creatively or innovatively, beyond conventional norms or constraints.

In 1914, Sam Loyd's Cyclopedia of 5000 Puzzles, Tricks, and Conundrums, included a nine dot puzzle test that is often used today in management and business thinking courses: the goal is to draw through 9 dots (stacked 3 x 3) without lifting your pen and using only straight lines.

#thinkoutsidethebox

Square the Circle

Square the circle

To solve a highly difficult problem.

This cliché has roots in a classic math and geometry problem of drawing a square within a circle that is of equal area; using only a set number of steps and a compass.

#squarethecircle

Let's get the ball rolling

To start a project or process.

The phrase came into use during the 1700s with popular sports that involved a ball.

#gettheballrolling

All hands on deck

An urgent call for all employees to direct their full attention and effort to a project, usually with a quickly looming deadline.

Not surprisingly, this phrase was used on ships when members of a crew had to report on deck during emergencies.

#allhandsondeck

ELEPHANT IN THE ROOM

Elephant in the room

A major problem or dilemma that is avoided or delayed, usually due to the unwillingness of all parties to engage in discussion and/or due to delicate political circumstances.

In Zambia, the Mfuwe Lodge, a 5 star safari lodge is known for its reception lobby where a herd of wild elephants stroll thru during mango season.

#elephantintheroom

Low hanging fruit

Easily accessible opportunities or wins.

This phrase is often used in investment banking, referring to a client who is willing to trust his/her assets to a bank.

#lowhangingfruit

Par for the course

An average result, typically with a gain and a loss.

This phrase is commonly used in golf and refers to a player's average or normal performance on a course.

#par4thecourse

on my plate

On my plate

What someone has on their schedule, agenda, project list. Typically used to communicate one's inability to take on additional projects e.g. "I've got too much on my plate."

We don't know where this came from but if we had to venture a guess, we would say it probably came from one too many office birthday parties where someone piled on too much sheet cake onto a tiny paper plate.

#onmyplate

Take it offline

A request or mandate to defer a discussion to a later time; usually in a private, less formal setting.

Yet another phrase from the IT world that has been adapted for more common use in everyday corporate slang. Originally, "taking it offline" meant being off your computer network. The phrase also has a more technical definition in computer science; referring to a process that occurs outside of a central processor.

#takeitoffline

I'm in the weeds

To be caught up in a difficult or messy situation, usually involving mind numbing details, bureaucratic inefficiencies or too many demands or requests, simultaneously.

Commonly (and somewhat surprisingly) used in the restaurant industry to describe a situation of a server or chef falling behind on too many orders.

#intheweeds

Back to the drawing board

A call to start over, usually following a failure or unsuccessful course of action.

This phrase may have originated from a 1941 New Yorker cartoon by artist Peter Amo whose cartoon depicted a plane crash and someone walking away, carrying blueprints saying "well, back to the drawing board." Unlike most clichés on this list, this one isn't too far removed from its literal roots.

#back2thedrawingboard

Let's touch base

A request to communicate or connect at a later time or place to discuss an important matter.

It's not entirely clear where this cliché came from. There are several theories on its origin: 1) baseball, a sport that involves running towards and touching bases before reaching home plate (or home base), 2) the military, where soldiers are expected or ordered to communicate with commanders at bases to provide status updates, 3) the world of music, specifically bass guitar and the idea that the bass player is a central figure in trios or ensembles.

#letstouchbase

#CorporateCliches

bemovingforward.com/coloringbook

Twitter: @bemovingforward
Facebook: /bemovingforward
LinkedIn: /company/be-moving-forward

Trivia References and Resources

A lot of the inspiration for this book came from the combined years that we, the authors, spent in corporate America. We also did some research (ahem Google!) to learn more about these corporate clichés. In doing so we found some amazing websites that we encourage you to check out, if you want to learn more. The only trivia we made up was for "on my plate" since it's not clear where this one came from. However, considering that we've been to a fair number of office birthday parties, we're pretty confident in our guess!

- www.answers.yahoo.com
- www.dictionary.com
- en.oxforddictionaries.com
- www.english.stackexchange.com
- www.idioms.thefreedictionary.com
- www.knowyourphrase.com
- www.phrases.org.uk
- www.programmerinterview.com
- www.reference.com
- www.smithsonianchannel.com
- www.vocabulary.com
- www.wikipedia.org
- Field research: spending many years in corporate America - behind cubicles, in meetings, on conference calls, at retreats, dressing down on casual Fridays and of course, attending numerous holiday and office birthday parties.
- Boersma, C. (2011, July). Let's touch base. Or was that basis? Intelligent Instinct. Retrieved from http://intelligentinstinct.blogspot.com/2011/07/lets-touch-baseor-was-that-bass.html.
- Doss, H. (2014, March). Does synergy really mean anything? Forbes. Retrieved from http://www.forbes.com/sites/henrydoss/2014/03/24/does-synergy-really-mean-anything/#64db411525c1.
- Weinstein, P., Peterson, W., Katz.,G. (Producers), & Peterson, W. (Director). (2000). The perfect storm [Motion Picture]. United States: Warner Bros. Pictures.

Made in the USA
Middletown, DE
09 December 2019